Ciara

by Z.B. Hill

Superstars of Hip-Hop

Ciara

by Z.B. Hill

Mason Crest

Ciara

Mason Crest
370 Reed Road
Broomall, Pennsylvania 19008
www.masoncrest.com

Printed and bound in the United States of America.

First printing
9 8 7 6 5 4 3 2 1

Library of Congress Cataloging-in-Publication Data

Hill, Z. B.
  Ciara / by Z.B. Hill.
    p. cm. – (Superstars of hip hop)
  Includes index.
  ISBN 978-1-4222-2513-4 (hardcover) – ISBN 978-1-4222-2508-0 (series hardcover) – ISBN 978-1-4222-9215-0 (ebook)
  1. Ciara (Vocalist)–Juvenile literature. 2. Singers–United States–Biography–Juvenile literature. I. Title.
  ML3930.C47H55 2012
  782.42164092–dc22
    [B]
                          2011005427

Produced by Harding House Publishing Services, Inc.
www.hardinghousepages.com
Interior Design by MK Bassett-Harvey.
Cover design by Torque Advertising & Design.

Publisher's notes:
 • All quotations in this book come from original sources and contain the spelling and grammatical inconsistencies of the original text.
 • The Web sites mentioned in this book were active at the time of publication. The publisher is not responsible for Web sites that have changed their addresses or discontinued operation since the date of publication. The publisher will review and update the Web site addresses each time the book is reprinted.

DISCLAIMER: The following story has been thoroughly researched, and to the best of our knowledge, represents a true story. While every possible effort has been made to ensure accuracy, the publisher will not assume liability for damages caused by inaccuracies in the data, and makes no warranty on the accuracy of the information contained herein. This story has not been authorized nor endorsed by Ciara.

Contents

Hip-Hop lingo

Each year, the National Academy of Recording Arts and Sciences gives out the **Grammy Awards** (short for Gramophone Awards)—or Grammys—to people who have done something really big in the music industry.

The word **celebs** is short for "celebrities," or famous people.

When someone has been **nominated**, she has been picked as one of the people who might win an award.

A **duet** is a song performed by two people.

R&B stands for "rhythm and blues." It's a kind of music that African Americans made popular in the 1940s. It has a very strong beat. Today, it's a style of music that's a lot like hip-hop.

Artists are people who create something. Some artists use their voices to make music.

Lyrics are the words in a song.

Mainstream music is music enjoyed by almost everyone.

A **revolution** happens when things suddenly change, or take a whole new direction.

Chapter 1

The First Lady of Crunk & B

It was the night of the 48th **Grammy Awards**. The setting sun glittered on the buildings of Los Angeles. Outside the Staples Center, the crowd buzzed as they waited for the **celebs** to appear.

Cameras flashed as a young woman stepped out of a car. She wore a beautiful white dress. She also wore a rhinestone belt that shimmered with every step. Her hair was pulled back to show her pretty, smiling face. Ciara had arrived at the Grammys!

It was a huge night for the young star. She had been on the music scene for less than two years. Nobody thought she could rise to the top so quickly. But she did. Now, she had been **nominated** for four Grammy Awards!

She had been nominated for Best New Artist, Best Rap/Sung Collaboration, Best Rap Song, and Best Short Form Music Video. At first, Ciara hadn't even believed it was true. She told *Rolling Stone* about the day she found out about the nomination. "I looked at my pager, and one of my old friends e-mailed me and said, 'Congratulations on your nomination.' And I was like, 'Huh? What nomination?'"

Ciara won the award for Best Short Form Music Video. She had also been asked to sing during the show—a huge honor! She changed from her long white dress into a tight black one. Then she sang a **duet** with Adam Levine from Maroon 5. They sang a song called "Everyday People."

"Everyday People" is a good song to describe Ciara. After all, just a few years before that night, she was far from famous. Ciara says that she hasn't changed. She's still just an "everyday person."

"I'm not a Barbie," she told *Rolling Stone*. "I'm just a regular around-the-way girl. I keep it cool. Keep it real."

Ciara's dad and mom both served in the army. Like most military families, they moved around a lot. Ciara went from one army base to another. She never stayed in one place long enough to make friends. But she did have music. From a young age, music helped her get through those hard times. When her family moved to Atlanta, she was ready to take that love to the next level.

Hip-hop and the music it influenced didn't stay in New York City, or even on the East and West coasts. It found its way to Atlanta, Georgia, where a young girl was growing—Ciara.

Crunk & B: Let's Dance!

Ciara's style combines music from **R&B**, hip-hop, and crunk. Crunk is a lot like hip-hop, with some important differences. Hip-hop **artists** talk about a lot of different things. They make music about anything from street life to politics. Crunk has a smaller focus. It usually has simple **lyrics** and a fast, heavy beat. The goal of crunk is to get people on the dance floor.

Crunk began in the 1980s, but it only went **mainstream** in the early 2000s. Lil Jon helped make crunk popular. He gave the heavy bass beats a lighter touch. That made them better for dancing in clubs. He called his new blend "Crunk & B." It's crunk with a little R&B thrown in. Together with Ciara and Usher, Lil Jon brought in a crunk **revolution**. He told Artist Direct, "Crunk & B songs are R&B songs that get you crunk. They make you wanna wild out."

Even so, Ciara does not think of herself as a crunk artist. Yes, crunk made her famous, but she says her style goes beyond just crunk. Her unique style is seen in her nicknames. She's been called the Princess, Ci Ci, and the Princess of Crunk & B. Lil Jon called her "The First Lady of Crunk & B."

Dreams Come True

Ciara's fame wasn't luck. She worked hard to get where she is today. Her hard work paid off. "I've been living my dream," she told her official website, CiaraWorld.com. "Everything has been great—winning a Grammy, having my first single go to No. 1, being named 'Entertainer of the Year' at the Soul Train Awards."

Even with all her success, she hasn't slowed down. Ciara seems to be unstoppable. But where did it all begin? Who is this "everyday" girl?

Hip-Hop lingo

Melodies are the tunes in a piece of music. They are made by arranging musical notes in a pattern.

A **professional** is someone who gets paid money to do something she's good at.

To **sacrifice** is to give up something in hopes of getting something else.

A **demo** is a rough, early version of a CD before the real thing comes out.

A **producer** is the person in charge of putting together songs. A producer makes the big decisions about the music.

A **label** is a company that produces music and sells CDs.

A **contract** is a written agreement between two people. Once you've signed a contract, it's against the law to break it. When a musician signs a contract with a music company, the musician promises to give all her music to that company for them to produce as CDs and then sell—and the music company promises to pay the musician a certain amount of money. Usually, a contract is for a certain period of time.

A Little Girl with a Big Dream

Ciara Princess Harris was born on October 25, 1985, in Austin, Texas. Both her parents served in the military. Her mother served in the air force and her father in the army. The family moved around a lot. Ciara lived on army bases in Germany, New York, California, Arizona, and Nevada. That didn't make it easy for a young girl to make friends.

The family finally settled in Atlanta, Georgia, when Ciara was in her early teens. She was happy to stop moving around.

The Dream Begins

Ciara's parents knew their daughter would do great things. At a young age, she has what it takes to succeed. She knew how to stick with things. She also had an interest in music. Her mother says that Ciara would sing every song she heard on the radio. She knew the words and the **melodies** by heart. As she got older, her love for music grew.

Even so, Ciara had other plans. At first, she wanted to be a model, not a singer. She put all her energy into that dream. Then, one day she saw Destiny's Child on TV. The group looked like they were having so much fun, dancing and singing for the crowd. That's when everything changed for Ciara. She told Artist Direct, "That's when I made up my mind: 'Hey, I wanna do this.'"

Jazze Pha knows real talent, and he saw it in young Ciara. He signed her to his record label when she was just sixteen. The producer turned out to be

Mainstream music seemed to lack really good dance music, and that was where Ciara excelled. Her music and live performances brought people to their feet, keeping them dancing song after song.

She started to focus on singing. She decided to put her dream into words. "I wrote down on paper that I had a goal to be a **professional** singer and I wanna be there soon. . . . I had to **sacrifice** a lot of things and I think that was the key thing to get me there."

Most teens live for the moment. They have a hard time planning for the future because it seems so far away. Not Ciara. She told her official website: "I cut out going to the movies. I cut out hanging with friends. I actually told some of my friends. . . . I cut out the boyfriend. . . ."

Stepping Stones

Ciara decided it was time to take some action. She teamed up with two other young singers to form a girl group. They performed in Atlanta, so Ciara was close to home. The group made a few **demos** but not much else. After six months, Ciara decided to go her own way. She didn't leave empty-handed though. She learned a lot from her time in the group. She got some good experience singing and dancing in front of a crowd.

Ciara also worked on her songwriting while in the group. When she was fifteen, she even started writing lyrics for other artists! She wrote lyrics for Mya and the famous singer Blue Cantrell. But her main goal stayed the same. She wanted to hear her own voice on the radio.

When she was sixteen, she met **producer** Jazze Pha. The two liked each other right away. In 2002, after working with her for only five days, Jazze signed Ciara to his Sho' Nuff **label**. Ciara's career was on track now. Jazze knew that Ciara could be a star. He wanted to help her get there. "God really put him in my life for a reason," she told Artist Direct.

High School Years

Ciara went to North Clayton High School in Atlanta. She kept up her studies while she worked on her career. She was on the track team for relays, the long jump, and the triple jump. She loved to compete. Then she changed schools again. This time she joined the cheerleading squad. Cheerleading was another chance for Ciara to perform in front of a crowd.

Despite her growing music career, Ciara also had a well-rounded high school career. She was a track star and cheerleader, and both of those activities helped her perform as a music star. Her classmates voted her "Most Likely to Become Famous."

It's not all glitz and glamour for Ciara. Though she has to get all dressed up for the increasing number of award shows and premieres she has to attend, she's like most people her age—she loves her jeans.

Even though she moved around a lot, Ciara was popular at school. She felt comfortable around people. Her classmates saw her talents. She was voted "Most Likely to Become Famous" in the yearbook! Ciara tried to keep her head in a good place. She had her sights set on bigger things than high school fame. On her website, she said the people her age were too worried about clothes and whether people liked them. "I was like, 'I'm trying to be some-body. What can I do to get there as soon as possible?'"

In 2003, Ciara graduated from Riverdale High School. The next year, Jazze Pha helped her get a **contract** with LaFace Records. Just like that, the dream had begun to become a reality.

Hip-Hop lingo

An **album** is a group of songs collected together on a CD.
Collaborators are two or more people who work together on a project.
In music, a **single** is one song sold by itself. It is its own CD.
An album goes **gold** when it sells more than 500,000 copies.
An album goes **platinum** when it sells more than 1,000,000 copies.
A **tour** means to travel around and play music for people at concerts.
An **idol** is someone looked up to with great respect.

Chapter 3

A Rising Star

Ciara was close to making her dream come true. But she still had work to do. She had a contract with a major label, but that didn't mean instant success. She didn't want to make a good **album**—she wanted to make a GREAT album. She wanted to become a hip-hop star. To do that, she would need great dance moves, a fresh image, and the best **collaborators**. And she would need a hit song.

It's Goodies to Be on Top

Ciara began work on another demo. She found that writing songs by herself was hard. She knew what she wanted to say. She wanted to be seen as a strong woman, but she didn't know how to say that in a song. The producers at LaFace saw that Ciara had talent. They decided she just needed a little help. So they called in Sean Garrett.

Garrett had helped Usher write his hit single "Yeah." He was a skilled producer. He and Ciara began to write the song "Goodies." They made it as a response to a song called "Freek-a-Leek" by Petey Pablo. In "Freek-a-Leek," Pablo says he wants women just for sex.

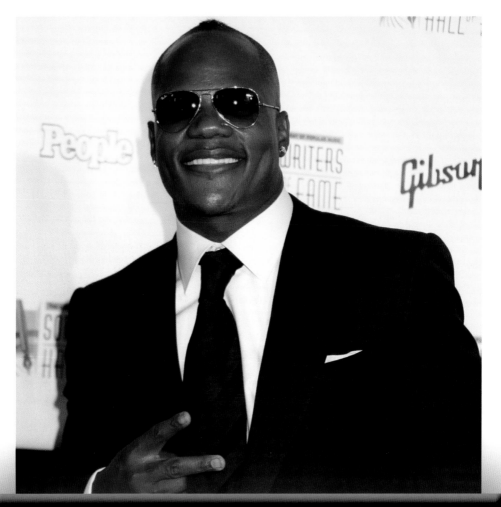

Collaboration is an important aspect of hip-hop and Crunk & B. So is a big hit. So, when Ciara needed to jump-start her career, she brought in one of the best, Sean Garrett. It worked. Ciara was on her way to stardom.

Ciara and Garrett wrote "Goodies" to say that women control their own bodies.

When it was done, they gave the demo to Lil Jon. He knew right away it was very good. So LaFace made the song a **single** in the summer of 2004. It was an instant hit! People loved Ciara's simple message. They liked her one-of-a-kind style. The song stayed at number one in the United States for seven weeks. By November, "Goodies" went **gold**. By January of 2005, it was **platinum**.

"Goodies" is a song about women taking back power. Ciara says that she won't give in to a man just because he's rich or good-looking. Ciara used the song to turn the table on men. She said, "I'm kind of putting it down like a guy would. This time it's in my control: 'This is what I want you to do.'"

When Lil Jon (right) heard Ciara's demo, he knew that a huge star was about to take off. He was so sure, that he produced the song. And when it debuted, he was proved right—it rocketed to #1 and stayed there for seven weeks.

Soon Ciara was showing up everywhere. She was a regular at award shows and red-carpet events. Fans and the paparazzi couldn't seem to get enough of the young star. Her talents were new, fresh, and hot.

The music video for "Goodies" told the same story. In it, Ciara wears a tiny black shirt that shows her stomach. Even so, women are not shown as sex objects. The video stays with the message of the song. Ciara is confident and sexy without giving in to men. The video also showed off Ciara's talent as a dancer.

First Album

Ciara's hit single made everyone excited about her first album. She called it *Goodies* after the popular song. In just over a month, the album went platinum! Some clubs wouldn't play Ciara's music. This was a safety issue—the crowds grew too wild when they heard her songs!

Goodies had three hit singles: "Goodies," "1, 2 Step," and "Oh." It turned out that Ciara has a great ear for what fans like. Some people told her not to keep "1, 2 Step." But Ciara knew the song had something special. She didn't listen to them. Her instinct turned out to be a good one. "1, 2 Step" became her second single. It went platinum too.

In the meantime, Ciara kept working with other artists. She was on Missy Elliott's track "Lose Control." She also sang with Bow Wow, who was her boyfriend for a while. They made a track together called "Like You." It was a busy time for Ciara. She loved it. Work kept coming in, and the young star kept rising higher.

On the Road

Being a star meant she had to be on the road a lot. In 2005, Ciara joined 50 Cent's The Massacre **Tour**. She was the only woman on stage. The rest were male hip-hop stars such as Lil Jon and Ludacris. Once again, Ciara proved to be a surprise! Many of the men she sang beside had been accused of treating women like sex objects. Ciara's music had the opposite message.

Being a hip-hop or Crunk & B star isn't all about bling. It's hard work, too. But Ciara wasn't afraid of the hard work, including the rigors of touring. She loves performing in front of her loyal fans.

Ciara had other big shows that year and the next. In January of 2006, she sang at one of the biggest football games in the country. Thousands of people were in the stands to watch the game. Millions of people watched on television. Ciara was nervous, but she put on a great show. The event only made her more famous.

Musical Idols

Since she was a little girl, Ciara has loved Janet and Michael Jackson. So she was very happy when people started comparing her to Janet. Ciara has tried to be like Janet since she started her career. She even dresses like Janet in her "Get Up" video. With her great dance music, some people think Ciara could be the "next Janet." Ciara says on her website that Janet is one of her **idols**. She says she has "so much respect for all she's done." She calls Janet's brother Michael her "inspiration."

Ciara's other idols are Madonna and Whitney Houston. And her favorite album is Tupac's *All Eyez on Me*. She admires these men and women for how they've handled fame. Being a star isn't easy. When everyone's watching you, everyone sees when you mess up. Ciara told *Blender*, "People don't realize just how much pressure being famous brings. Especially when everybody turns on you."

Ciara admires her heroes' careers. She wants to make music that lasts, just like they did. There's no doubt that Ciara has her head in the right place. She's looking to learn lessons from the past so she can move into the future.

Hip-Hop lingo

Something that **inspired** a person gave him ideas and made him want to do something.

Records are groups of songs played on plastic discs by a phonograph. Today, a lot of people still call CDs and MP3s "records."

Critics are people who judge artistic works and say what is good and what is bad about them.

Positive means focusing on good things and believing that they can happen.

Abstinence means not having sex before marriage.

Pop is short for "popular." Pop music is usually light and happy, with a good beat.

Chapter 4

Taking That Next Step

Making *Goodies* was a step in the right direction for Ciara. It launched her career and made her famous. It was a fun album that got people dancing. But it wasn't very personal. It didn't really talk about the stuff that was most important to Ciara. So she decided to take it up a notch on the next album.

She called this album *Ciara: The Evolution*. The word "evolution" means to grow and change over time. This is exactly what had happened to Ciara. She had learned a lot in those short years in the music business. She said on her website, "I've learned so much and I feel like I've continued to get better with everything I've done in the last two years." She also thanked some people, saying, "I've been blessed to have friends and family. . . . I appreciate all that has happened and now I feel like I'm going to a whole new place with my evolution in fashion, dance, and in my music."

Her next album definitely took her "to a whole new place." This time, Ciara didn't have to look around for people to help her. They came to her! Everyone wanted to work with the talented young singer.

Jazze Pha, Rodney Jerkins, Pharrell, and will.i.am all offered to help. Ciara had the final say on how the songs would sound, though. She loved to have guest artists on her albums. But she didn't let them overpower her own sound. "They spice a record; they add a little seasoning to it. I'm the dressing, and they put a little gravy on it."

Another Big Hit

Ciara pushed hard to build excitement for *Evolution*. Before the album came out, she went on tour. She sang songs from the new CD. People loved them! The stage was set for another big hit.

It didn't take long. The album had three singles. They were "Get up," "Promise," and "Like a Boy." Ciara added a DVD to the CD. It had over thirty minutes of music videos and dance moves. It even showed fans how to do some of the dance moves. *Evolution* was a smash hit.

Ciara was happy with the album she'd made. She said on her MySpace page, "A lot of the music on this album was **inspired** by old school **records**. There was a way music used to feel and I wanted to capture that. . . . All I know is, it feels good with my soul!"

Some **critics** didn't think Ciara should be so pleased. They said that true R&B fans didn't listen to Ciara. They said her lyrics and voice were weak.

Well, whether they're "true" R&B fans or not, one thing is for sure: there are a lot of them. *Evolution* sold over 338,000 copies in the first week!

Girl Power

Ciara kept up the **positive** message for women. "Goodies" told women not to give in to men. Her new song, "Like a Boy," pointed

Evolution might have contained more ballads than her previous release, but Ciara didn't forget the fans who wanted to dance. It also included numbers guaranteed to get people moving, just as Ciara does in her concerts. It's enough to tire out anyone!

out that men and women are not treated as equals. She said our society accepts it when men cheat on women. But if a woman does the same thing, she's called bad names. The song also said that men get away with treating women poorly. Ciara wanted women to stand up for themselves.

Ciara also believes that women should not sleep around. Ciara stands out from a lot of hip-hop artists. She believes in **abstinence**. She told *Blender*, "I'm not totally innocent, and I do date. But as a young woman, I also demand respect. . . . Sex before marriage—it's not right."

Ciara is one of the only hip-hop artists to send this message. Since it began, men have mostly controlled hip-hop. It's hard enough for a woman to make it big in hip-hop. It makes it even harder when she doesn't want to be a sex object for men.

But Ciara has done it with style and grace. She wears clothes that are form fitting. She doesn't hide her body. But she doesn't believe that women are only useful when they're pleasing men. Her songs say that women and men are equal. They say that both should be treated with respect.

Ciara on the Big Screen

Ciara has also acted in movies. She decided to try acting and found she had some talent. In 2006, she starred in a movie called *All You've Got*. It was about two high school volleyball teams. They have to work together after one team's school burns down. The message of the movie was positive, like Ciara's music. It tells people not to fight. It says that we all have a lot in common.

In 2010, Ciara starred in *Mama, I Want to Sing!* Ciara plays a preacher's daughter. She sings in the church choir. One day, James Brown hears her sing. He helps the young girl become a **pop** star. It was a great role for Ciara. The story of the preacher's daughter

Okay, Ciara's a music powerhouse and an up-and-coming actress, so what more could she do? The answer, of course, is to become a fashion icon. Ciara has earned a reputation for her sense of style.

Ciara takes her responsibility toward young people very seriously. She wants boys and girls, men and women, to have the same opportunities. These ideas have made her popular with young fans, including those who vote in the Nickelodeon Kid's Choice Awards.

was a lot like Ciara's own story. She too followed her dreams and became a star. Ciara acts in movies like *Mama* for a reason. She hopes it will inspire kids to follow their own dreams.

Awards

Fans around the world can't get enough of Ciara. And it's not only the fans who see her talent. She has been given many awards for her work. She received the Pop Music Awards for songwriting, Teen Choice Awards, BET Awards, MTV Music Video Awards, Soul Train Lady of Soul Music Awards, Vibe Awards, and Grammy Awards.

But she hasn't let it go to her head. *Rolling Stone* asked her what she would do if she won a Grammy. She said, "This may sound a little weird to you, but I'm a simple person. My after-Grammy party is me and all my people hanging together, at the hotel. Then I'm gonna celebrate by making more hit **records**."

Ciara is happy about her success. She is thankful she's won so many awards. She's found many ways to use her fame for good. But all the attention has its downside, too. As Ciara has reached the top of fame, she's had to deal with many hateful rumors.

Hip-Hop lingo

A **co-writer** is someone who writes something with another person.

A **role model** is someone to whom kids can look up and try to be like.

Charity is doing something to help make people's lives better.

Motivation is what makes a person want to do something.

The **media** is the group of people who create news. Media can be photographs, videos, or news articles.

Tracks are parts—usually songs—of an album.

Chapter 5

Behind the Pretty Face

Ciara likes to keep it real. Being a celebrity can tempt a person to behave differently. She says she hasn't changed, though. She doesn't let the fame go to her head. She told thabiz.com, "You know, I'm pretty much the same person. I take it for what it is. I love the fans. I appreciate it."

She doesn't let anyone tell her who to be or how to act. She controls her own image. She told *Rolling Stone*, "Whenever I sing about anything, I think it's important that it's something I can relate to, something I believe in." Many hip-hop artists let other people write their songs. Not Ciara. She always wants a say. She is a **co-writer** or co-producer on most of her songs.

Becoming famous at a young age has other dangers. Many young artists get caught up in drugs or alcohol. Again—not Ciara. She doesn't want to be one of those people. "I don't drink," she told *Rolling Stone*. "I'm a crazy person, though. I get that natural high."

Ciara says she was raised with strict religious beliefs. Those same beliefs still guide her life today. Ciara wants to use her fame to make people's lives better. "I believe I was placed in front of millions of people for a reason," she told *Blender*. "People look up to me, they see me as their **role model**, and that's cool."

Showing Some Love

Ciara is a busy person. But even so, she takes time to help others. **Charity** work is very important to her. She picks causes she cares about. In 2005, she sang at the Christmas in Washington concert. The event raised money for the National Children's Hospital. Many important people were there, even the President!

Earlier that year, Hurricane Katrina had struck. It destroyed a lot of homes. Being from Atlanta, Ciara didn't live far from the worst-hit areas. She worked with *Vibe* magazine to raise money for victims. She also recorded two songs to help raise even more money.

In 2006, she sang at the 4th Annual VH1 Save the Music Hamptons Benefit. The goal was to raise money for music programs in public schools. In total, they raised over $500,000! Ciara was very excited to do the benefit. She strongly believes in giving music to kids. After all, music is the love of her life. It's what made her famous.

Ciara's biggest focus is on helping kids. One of her charities is called Give a Smile. It helps kids with bad teeth get braces. The goal is to make kids proud of their smile.

Ciara loves children. In 2008, she told About.com her plans to be a mother one day: "To be honest, that's part of the **motivation** for everything that I do. There's so much more that I need to accomplish in my career before I have kids. So I'm motivated by the idea of having kids and a family. I wanna work as hard as I can right now, so that when I do choose to start a family, I can do it comfortably and spend time with them."

Like many music artists, Ciara does her best to give back to her community and to the world. One of her causes is VH1's Save the Music. In this photo, she is shown performing at one of the benefit concerts.

Imagine trying to have a relationship with your boyfriend or girlfriend with screaming photographers and paparazzi in your face most of the time. When Ciara dated Bow Wow, they were the subject of a lot of gossip, much of it hurtful. That's a downside of fame.

The Downside of Fame

Famous people deal with a lot of attention. They always have people chasing them down for photos. Or reporters trying to find out about their private lives. Ciara has struggled with nasty rumors in the **media**.

For a while, Ciara dated the rapper Bow Wow. One day, he bought Ciara a large diamond ring. It was just a present, not a wedding ring. But people began saying that the two were engaged. The couple had to explain that they weren't getting married. Then, a year later, the media said that Bow Wow was cheating on Ciara. He had been spotted in L.A. with another woman. But this, too, was confusing the truth. Bow Wow and Ciara had actually broken up a few months before. There were no hard feelings. Bow Wow was free to date other people. Ciara wished him the best of luck.

It can be hard to lead a normal life when you're famous!

Still Making Music

Ciara released her third album in 2009. She called it *Fantasy Ride*. Once again, people loved Ciara's sound. **Critics** praised her for taking her sound to the next level.

A few songs had great success. "Never Ever" and "Work" became huge hits. People were surprised to see Ciara continue to get better. Unlike some stars, who disappear after a few years on the scene, Ciara kept going strong.

In 2010, Ciara released **tracks** from her next album, *Basic Instinct*. She released "Ride," "Speechless," and "Gimmie Dat." *Basic Instinct* didn't sell very well. Ciara said that the low sales weren't a problem. But her label saw things differently. Soon, Jive Records stopped working with Ciara. The young singer had no record label and needed a new one.

It's hard to believe that Ciara has come so far so quickly.
But if you listen to her songs, you'll see why. Unlike others who have shot
to stardom quickly, only to crash and burn shortly after, there's no sign that
Ciara's career won't continue to rise.

Not long after she was dropped from Jive, Ciara started working with a new record company, Epic Records. Epic is run by one of music's most famous businessmen, L.A. Reid. He said he saw plenty of talent in Ciara. Reid knew that Ciara could still be a big music star. She just needed the right company behind her.

Ciara started working on her next album. She told fans that she was going to take her time making the album. She wanted to make sure her new music was as good as it could be before she gave it to fans. No matter what Ciara put out next, many fans would be waiting!

Hard Work Paying Off

There seems to be no end to Ciara's musical flow. She just keeps making the music she loves. She just keeps working to make big hits and great albums. And the young star still has plenty of time to make more.

Ciara doesn't want to be just another singer. She wants her music to change people's lives. "It's not just about making clever lyrics and singing and dancing to a banging track," Ciara told Artist Direct. "My goal is to deliver a positive message and let people know they're not the only one going through things."

Ciara has worked hard and it's paid off. She has a lot of options in her life right now. She might decide to be a mom or keep making hit songs—or both. The choice is hers to make.

1940s   Rhythm and blues develops.

1970s   Hip-hop develops in the Bronx section of New York City.

1980s   Crunk originates in Memphis, Tennessee.

Oct. 25, 1985
Ciara is born in Austin, Texas.

2002   Ciara signs with the record label Sho' Nuff.

2003   Ciara graduates from Riverdale High School.

2004   Ciara signs with LaFace Records.

2004   Ciara's first single, "Goodies" is released and hits Number 1; it is certified gold in November.

2004   Ciara becomes the first female artist to release a Crunk & B single.

Sept. 28, 2004
Ciara's debut album is released; it is certified platinum in November.

2005   Ciara is the only female artist to perform on 50 Cent's The Massacre Tour.

April 2005
"1, 2 Step" is certified platinum, and "Goodies" is certified multi-platinum.

July 2005
Ciara releases a DVD, *Goodies: The Videos & More.*

Dec. 2005
Ciara performs at the Christmas in Washington concert.

Dec. 9, 2005
Ciara ranks ninth on Yahoo!'s annual list of the most searched-for names on the Internet.

2006 Ciara wins a Grammy Award and performs at the ceremony.

Jan. 2006
Ciara performs at the half-time show of the Orange Bowl.

May 2006
Ciara makes her acting debut in *All You've Got*.

July 2006
Ciara performs at the 4th Annual VH1 Save the Music Hamptons Benefit.

Oct. 2006
Ciara performs at the This Day Music Festival in Nigeria.

Dec. 5, 2006
Ciara's second album, *Ciara: The Evolution*, debuts at Number 1.

May 2007
Ciara becomes the new face of Rocawear clothing line.

May 11, 2007
Ciara announces that she will host Glamour's Reel Music contest.

Aug.–Sept. 2007
Ciara tours with BET's Scream Tour, Screamfest '07.

2009 Ciara releases *Fantasy Ride*.

2010   Ciara releases *Basic Instinct.*

2011   Ciara stars in *Mama, I Want to Sing!*

Ciara is dropped from Jive Records.

Ciara signs to Epic Records to begin work on her fifth studio album.

Discography

Albums

2004   Goodies

2006   Ciara: The Evolution

2009   Fantasy Ride

2010   Basic Instinct

DVDs

2005   Goodies: Videos and More

Books

Baker, Soren. *The History of Rap and Hip Hop*. San Diego, Calif.: Lucent, 2006.

Comissiong, Solomon W. F. *How Jamal Discovered Hip-Hop Culture*. New York: Xlibris, 2008.

Cornish, Melanie. *The History of Hip Hop*. New York: Crabtree, 2009.

Czekaj, Jef. *Hip and Hop, Don't Stop!* New York: Hyperion, 2010.

Haskins, Jim. *One Nation Under a Groove: Rap Music and Its Roots*. New York: Jump at the Sun, 2000.

Hatch, Thomas. *A History of Hip-Hop: The Roots of Rap*. Portsmouth, N.H.: Red Bricklearning, 2005.

Web Sites

Ciara
www.popstarplus.com/music_ciara.htm

Ciara Official Web Site
www.ciaraworld.com

Ciara on MySpace
www.myspace.com/ciara

Index

About the Author

Z.B. Hill is a an author and publicist living in Binghamton, New York. He has a special interest in adolescent education and how music can be used in the classroom.

Picture Credits